Black Pain

Black Pain

Charles Spencer

To order additional copies of this book, contact:
Xlibris Corporation
1-888-795-4274
www.Xlibris.com
Orders@Xlibris.com
47850

Before I introduce myself I would like to thank God for blessing me with the ability to compose this literature. I would like to thank my mother Margaret Yvonne James for having faith in supporting this book.

My name is Charles Spencer A.K.A. (Yum) and I am the author of Black Pain. Black Pain was spawned from the trials and tribulations that plague the black community and now this pain has reached a multitude of cultures in today's society. When you read this literature please read with your family and loved ones and keep an open mind to the contents of what you are reading. I strongly believe with an open mind will enable you to relate to some if not all of my poetry and enjoy as much as I enjoyed creating it.

My heart is broken it can't be fixed
I can remember hating life since the age of six
Most of time I stay to myself and was content
Being alone
It seemed like yesterday when I ran away from home
I came back fast cause it was dark and I was afraid
Dreaming of the day when I could get paid
That dream never happened so I constantly live a nightmare
Sometimes feeling upset my father wasn't there
God got me through you can't miss what you never had
But I can't help sometimes for feeling sad

I remember when we use to meet in the park
We wouldn't get home until dark
It seemed like magic was in the air
I enjoyed the love that we shared
Just say you will always be mine
Baby you're one of a kind
If you were lost you would be easy to find
My love I will always love you until the end of time

*BLACK PAIN IS HATING THE CHOICES
YOU MADE
BLACK PAIN IS USING ALCOHOL AS YOUR
AIDE
BLACK PAIN IS COMPARING LIFE AND
DEATH
BLACK PAIN IS SOMEONE TAKING YOUR
LAST BREATH
BLACK PAIN IS NO RESPECT FOR
AUTHORITY
BLACK PAIN IS WHEN DRUGS BECOME
PRIORITY
BLACK PAIN IS ALWAYS FEELING OLD
BLACK PAIN IS NEVER DOING WHAT
YOURE TOLD
BLACK PAIN IS NOT BELIEVING IN A
POWER HIGHER THAN YOU
BLACK PAIN IS WHEN REALITY BECOMES
TRUE*

I hate going through this pain
At times, I feel like cutting my vanes
Often I feel insane
I wish know one knew my name
It is very hard out here
That is why I drank so much beer
Crying until I shed tears
Hoping someone could understand my fears
Praying to make it through the year
Wishing god will bring me cheer

Black Pain is when your thoughts are bare
Black Pain is when no one cares
Black Pain is crying yourself to sleep
Black Pain is not having anything to eat
Black Pain is having to bath in a river
Black Pain is having cerosis of the liver
Black Pain is when you always tell a lie
Black Pain is feeling like you want to die

Black pain is having a car that won't start

Black pain is having a broken heart

Black pain is only having a third grade education

Black pain is having no graduation

Black pain is ambition with no dedication

Black pain is my bad luck situation

Black pain is segregation

Black pain has ruin the nation

Black pain is having a president that don't care

Black pain is having no love to share

Black pain is your ceiling being someone else's floor

Black pain is accepting the fact of being poor

Black pain is killing to even the score

Black pain is after dinner wanting more

Black pain is having to steel and rob

Black pain is not having a job

Black pain is wanting to be white

Black pain is being higher than a kite

Black pain is hating your neighbor

Black pain is having to do hard labor

Black pain is having your vehicle reposed

Black pain is having to confess

Black pain is hoping for no tomorrow

Black pain is having to find money to borrow

Black pain is living in the commonwealth

BLACK pain is when the doctor says you have bad health

Black pain is hurting on the inside

Black pain is being an outcast worldwide

Black pain is always being called the bad guy

Black pain is when one calls you shy

Black pain is feeling like you living in hell

Black pain is having to live in a jail cell

Black pain is not knowing whom to call your friend

Black pain is not being able to count to ten

Black pain is when the school system has let you down

Black pain is when your parents are not around

Black pain is when it is difficult to learn

Black pain is when you steel instead of earn

Black pain is when you cannot tell someone how you feel

Black pain is when you cannot determine what is real

Black pain is having mouths to feed
Black pain is having books and cant read
Black pain is having to eat porknbeans and hotdogs everyday
Black pain is having stomach pains that wont go away
Black pain is crying about shedding no more tears
Black pain is not having any good years
Black pain is having dreams you cant achieve
Black pain is in the winter wearing a shirt with no sleeves

This is a sad world that we live in
Don't be foolish the government isn't your friend
Always trying to make up for the past
But keeping the minority best interest last
Its hard living in a society that hates me cause the color of my skin
Will the ignorance in their mind ever end
A lot of things say in GOD we trust
But what about the humanity they took from us
If GOD is our saver then is he also our supplier
If this to be true I suppose my history teacher was a liar

I don't know why I drink
Could it be my life stinks
Feeling like it wont get any better
There is no happiness in jail letters
It would be great if I were free
When I am released, will anyone remember me
Hate being locked up in this cage
Wishing I didn't have so much rage
Thinking of ways I can get paid
Dam I am so afraid

How can life be so sad
Trying to hold on to something you never had
Could things be any worst
Walking around feeling like you are cursed
Keep god in your life and you will be all right
Remember to say your prayers each night

If I told you, I miss you would you care
Or would you say get out my hair
We need each other as a car needs gas
No more images take off the mask
You know you love me, as if I love you
There isn't a love more powerful than ours and you know that to be true
The sun does not shine when you are gone
Without you in my life I feel I cant go on

Today is our anniversary and we have a lot to be thankful for
Being we have each other, we need nothing more
We celebrate being together and should never be apart
Wild horses could drag you out of heart
I thank god cause he made you for me
Two people loving one another is how it should be

They say Cain killed Abel
Does that mean we should fight at the kitchen table
Bless the food and lets eat
Remember life is so sweet
Love one another cause here today gone tomorrow
Everyone knows with death comes sorrow
Sometimes our feelings are not alone
Always keep love and peace inside our homes

Does anyone know how it feels to be alone
Or how it feels to come from a broken home
Do you often cry and wonder why
Have you ever hoped to die
Filled with so much emptiness in your heart
Asking yourself why this day have to start
Not knowing how it would end
Wishing you had a friend
Thanking GOD, you have hope
Remember you can't wash away your sins with soap

I LOVE YOU SO MUCH IT HURTS
IM SORRY FOR NOT HAVING A LOT OF PERKS
I NEED YOU I CANT LET YOU GO
I HOPED OUR LOVE WOULD GROW
I WILL ALWAYS BE YOUR MAN
I WILL LOVE YOU THE BEST I CAN

Kids are sent from heaven above
Most of our kids were made from love
Kids can be good or bad
Majority of our kids don't have dads
Hey, I guess you can't miss something you never had
So, don't spend your whole life being mad

You make me feel like nothing else matters
If you left my heart would shatter
I thank God for putting you in my life
Know one could ask for a better wife
You bring me joy when I am down
My world is wonderful when you are around
I just want to say thanks for you being you
With all my heart I love you and you know it's true

Woke up this morning feeling bad
All my life without a dad
My mother took great care of my sisters and me
She did a good job cant you see
She always said put God first
Now you tell me what a woman is worth
For she is the greatest, know one can compare
I like to thank God and my mom for giving me life to breath air

When you need me I will be there
This is a promise to you I swear
It doesn't matter what time it is I will be around
Even if I am across town
I will do anything to prove my love
Thank God you were sent from heaven above
Trust in me and take my hand
Baby I will love you the best I can

Did anyone tell you that they like your eyes
Baby I love you that's no surprise
Were going to make it through this love thing
Honey be my garden ill be your rain
THANK's for the love we made last night
Know matter what we will be alright
Always remember love shouldn't cost a thing
Soon I will give you a wedding ring
Hold on to me as I will hold on to you
Were stuck together like glue

It's hard to get romance
When you have no finance
Sometimes just do your best
One day you might find success
These days are hard times
How else could I come up with these rhymes
We all need things to strive for
Can a person help it if they are poor

Even though times are hard, we will be all right
If we keep saying our prayers through the day and night
We are going to make it, we wont always be broke
Just remember there's always hope
With GOD as our provider, we do not have to worry about a thing
For he is responsible for everything

Life is good when you do what you should
We don't have to live in the hood
But what about that child that gets stuck
Meanwhile selling drugs is his lifestyle to make a buck
Or is it cause his morals have been robbed
Could it be that his bills need to be paid
Maybe it's just a choice that he made
Educate our children so they wont be afaid
Teach them how to love instead of throwing a grenade

Nothing worse than doing hard time
They can enslave our body but not our mind
Learning about things that really doesn't matter
Everyday thinking about my dreams that I have shattered
Mad and confused cause I couldn't make bail
Because of bad choices I am in jail
The judge gave me life without parole
I would be free if only I would have did as I was told
My mother always taught me right from wrong
Now since I didn't listen my freedom is gone

I GOT OUT OF BED AND WAS FEELING DOWN
IT HURT SO BAD CAUSE YOU WASN'T AROUND
I WAS USE TO BEING IN YOUR ARMS
I NEVER MEANT TO CAUSE YOU ANY HARM
YOU CLAIMED YOU WOULD ALWAYS BE THERE
I NEVER THOUGHT THE DAY WOULD COME THAT YOU
    WOULDN'T CARE
COME BACK CAUSE I HATE US BEING APART
YOU WILL AWAYS BE CLOSE TO MY HEART

It's hard out here for a young black man that's trying to do right.
Three to four months in deep thought looking for some insight
I wont beg, steal or borrow. I will get off my ass keep trying to find a job
and hope not to drown deep in my sorrow
I hate the fact I was laid off but I have four mouths to feed.
Therefore, I must be strong cause it hurts to know my children
have seen me fail.
Days and nights, I cry not understanding why this world could be so cruel.
I ask my dear lord to save me cause it looks like I am headed for jail.
So many thoughts in my head and I cant think clearly wishing I could get
it together. Even though I have, my faith things still don't get any better
We take things for granted and in a matter of seconds, they are gone.
Talking to myself saying how long my bad situation must go on.
So I embrace myself and say today I cant take anymore.
I walk two blocks cause my car is reposed and I walk into a store.
Should I commit murder and rob the safe are the thoughts that crossed my
mind. Instead, I get on my knees and pray GOD please lead the way and
put all my bad thoughts behind.

Black pain is depending on drugs to survive
Black pain is cheating on your mate
Black pain is being a ward of the state
Black pain is feeling like a disgrace
Black pain is feeling out of place
Black pain is when you don't feel safe
Black pain is when you lack faith

Black pain is when your poverty level doesn't change
Black pain is asking for spare change
Black pain is knowing you wont survive
Black pain is wishing you wasn't alive
Black pain is hating every day above ground
Black pain is when you don't have any family around
Black pain is when you have no pride black pain is wanting to commit suicide

Black pain is living from check to check

Black pain is when a bill collector is ready to collect

Black pain is not being able to afford clothes

Black pain is trying to hide the truth from someone who knows

Black pain is only putting five dollars in your car for gas

Black pain is saying we finally made it at last

Black pain is not being able to handle your stress

Black pain is not knowing when you have done your best

Black pain is when you don't have money to pay the rent
Black pain is reaching into your pocket and coming out with lent
Black pain is when your dreams become nightmares
Black pain is when no one cares
Black pain is when you don't have food to eat
Black pain is when you hate everyone you meet
Black pain is when they say you fit the description
Black pain is not being happy without a prescription
Black pain is living in a world that hates your skin
Black pain is when God is your only friend

Black Pain is our soldiers over in Iraq
Black pain is the sadness of the ones whom won't return back
Black pain is the hatred in our society and nation
Black pain is that our Government is running the world like a plantation
Black pain is believing in the Red the White and the Blue
Black pain is failing when no matter how hard you try
Black pain is being in a war and not understanding the reason why

Black pain is when you loose the one you love
Black pain is when you don't believe there's a heaven above
Black pain is feeling like you don't have the strength to go on
Black pain is hating the fact that you were ever born
Black pain is knowing you will always be
Black pain is being a product of a broken home
Black pain is not knowing the difference between hell or heaven
Black pain is when you feel life is over at the age of seven

Black pain is my feelings and my thoughts
Black pain is filled with emotins that can't be brought
Black pain is how I feel from day to day
Black pain is a feeling that wont go away
Black pain can't be borrowed
Black pain can also be a felling of sorrow
Black pain is when you feel like taking your life with a sword
Black pain is realizing you need the lord

Black pain is not having what u need

Black pain is having books and can't read

Black pain is eating hotdogs and pork 'n beans everyday

Black pain is having stomach pains that won't go away

Black pain is crying but shedding no more tears

Black pain is having no good years

Black pain is having dreams you can't achieve

Today I am happy cause I am alive
Know one knows the feelings I have inside
I want to be love and happy for the rest of my life
I want god to bless me with a wonderful wife
I would treat her with kindness and care
I would let her know that I would always be there

I hate going through this pain
At times, I feel like cutting my vanes
Often I feel insane
I wish know one knew my name
It is very hard out here
That is why I drank so much beer
Crying until I shed tears
Hoping someone could understand my fears
Praying to make it through the year
Wishing God will bring me cheer

DON'T LET LIFE KEEP YOU DOWN
REMEMBER I WILL ALWAYS BE AROUND
YOU HAVE A LOT OF THINGS TO LOOK FORWARD TO
JUST DON'T FORGET I LOVE YOU
THANK YOU FOR BEING WHOM YOU ARE
HEAVEN IS WATCHING YOU FROM UP AFAR
SO YOU SHOULD ALWAYS HAVE A SMILE ON YOUR FACE
CAUSE GOD WILL KEEP YOU SAFE

Even though you left me, I still have my pride
I know I am a good man that's why it hurts inside
I gave you my heart cause I thought you were the best
Dam I didn't know you would fail the test
Everyday you bitched, argued and struck a nerve
I ran your bathwater, gave you candlelight dinners, cause I thought that's
     what you deserved
Thank GOD you are gone, cause I couldn't take anymore
I finally realized you wasn't a QUEEN, but a very big whore

Black pain is being in jail

Black pain is having no bail

Black pain is having no canteen

Black pain is being on drugs and called a phoene

Black pain is being locked up for nothing you have done

Black pain is your mother saying she doesn't have a son

Black pain is having to be alone

Black pain is calling someone from jail only getting the dial tone

I remembered when we first kissed
You're kitty Kat hissed
Oh how I never thought I could feel like this
Your beautiful body I miss
I wish I could hold you and squeeze you tight
If you were up against a lion, I would put up a fight
No one truly knows what you are worth
Just like god, I would put you first

Son am sorry I couldn't be there
You're grown up now but life isn't fair
I tried my best to give you what I could
Please don't hate me cause I wasn't around like I should
Just believe in faith when things get better for me ill be there
Always remember daddy cares
Theres a lot of things we didn't get to do
God knows I will always love you

Black pain is missing your child first words
Black pain is feeling ushered
Black pain is when you feel that love doesn't matter
Black pain is when your heart has shattered
Black pain is alcoholism
Black pain is having no wisdom
Black pain is taking twelve steps back
Black pain is enjoy smoking crack
Black pain is not remembering your own name
Black pain is feeding poison to your brain

Someone once asked me why I wrote Black Pain
I told them it wasn't for fortune nor fame
I wrote cause of the things that wasn't right in my life
Also based on all those lonely nights
No one will ever know my experience of black pain
Cause my heart doesn't pump of blood but in vain
So many of years wanting to die
If you were to ask me, I couldn't say why
I keep my head up high looking for hope
Thanking my god for never trying dope

Manufactured By: RR Donnelley
                     Momence, IL USA
                     October, 2010